INTERLUDE

I had been meditating for a few hours and I kept hearing, "When the scars heal, transformation will come." I saw a caterpillar transform into a butterfly. I heard the Lord say, "We have to be properly healed in order for transformation to take place." We have allowed the sore to heal on the outside, but on the inside it's not healed. In order to go through transformation we have to go through the process. On the outside, it looks like we are healed; yet on the inside, it's still some unhealed places. In this hour, God is calling all of his people to properly heal. "Properly heal" is like, stuck in my mind.

Have you ever spent a period of your life fighting to become free of all the hurt and pain you caused yourself, or pain others inflicted upon you? Well, take a seat and let's explore this journey together. I can remember going from one phase (trial) to another. God would heal me from one issue, and boom, another issue comes to mind. I packed it away because at the time it was easier to say, "Forget it!", instead of dealing with it. Then one day you look around and all the things that made you sad, all the things that made you cry, all the things that made you stay awake at night worrying are now no longer an issue.

 It leaves you feeling lost or like you are trying to fit in; yet, you don't know where you belong. Sounds crazy, huh? When we begin to seek the plan or the will of God for our lives, we will understand that God will take all our mistakes and failures and turn them into something beautiful. Yes! It's possible when you allow God to uproot all the things that stop you from being prosperous in life.

We have to understand that it is a time and a season for everything that happens in our lives.

Ecclesiastes 3:3 say, "To everything there is a season, and a time to every purpose under heaven."Let's look at Ecclesiastes 3:4; it says, "A time to weep, and a time to laugh; a time to mourn, and a time to dance." Some of us have wept, mourned, grieved and cried; but it's a time to smile, laugh and dance.

I had to learn I was more than a survivor. Always in survivor mode, I stayed fighting to exist, fighting to catch up, trying to do the things I should have done while I was grieving, and trying to prove a point to myself kept me working twice as hard, leaving me feeling overworked and stressed. All I had to do was trust the will of God for my life.

BLUEPRINTS

We have to seek the will of God for our lives right now and not try to fulfill the plan we had before life blew up in our faces. Who are you now? What is the will for your life now? What is your God-given purpose now? The trials of life change us more than we could ever realize; yet, we try to live in a house that has been burned down.

It won't work! The Bible tells us to forget the former things. Isaiah 43:18-19 (NIV) says, "Forget the former things; do not dwell on the past. See, I am doing a new thing! Now it springs up; do you not perceive it? I am making a way in the wilderness and streams in the wasteland."

What is a blueprint? A blueprint is a guide for making something — it's a design or pattern that can be followed. (Dictionary.com) The Holy Bible is our blueprint Jesus left behind to be a set of instructions to help guide us in our day-to-day lives.

Isaiah 55:9 say, "As the heavens are higher than the earth, so are my ways higher than your ways and my thoughts than your thoughts." This is another way of God assuring us to follow the blueprints He has created just for our lives.

Why is a biblical blueprint important? A biblical blueprint allows you to design your life with the big picture in mind. In this way, you can ensure you reach every milestone and build consistency throughout your life. Even when faced with uncertainty, we can rest assured God is with us.

Ephesians 1:9-10 says, "He made known to us the mystery of His will according to His good pleasure, which He purposed in Christ, to be put into effect when the times reach their fulfillment to bring unity to all things in heaven and on earth under Christ." This simply means everything in heaven and on earth, past, present or future comes into crystal clear focus as we begin to live by the Grace of God.

Over and over throughout Paul's letter to the Ephesians, God is saying, "Walk this way." Our old life outside of Christ can be an example of what not to do in our new life in Christ. Our old life outside of Christ is no longer a roadblock to our new life in Christ. The second half of the letter is especially direct in showing us how to be imitators of God, as His beloved children. And we get to see all of these descriptions, commands, and encouragements through God's plan to connect all things in Christ.

TRANSFORMATION

Transformation, in its most awesome form, occurs from the inside out. A good example is the caterpillar turning into a butterfly type metamorphosis. A person who has transformed changes so dramatically that they can often be unrecognizable, either in their appearance or their character. We all understand the dramatic shift in appearance the caterpillar makes as it emerges from its chrysalis, but what about a person?

Romans 12 is full of information about the great love and mercy God pours upon His children. We often become confused when reading the passage about presenting "your bodies as a living sacrifice", and again when confronted with "be transformed by the renewal of your mind." What on earth is the scripture talking about? What is this living sacrifice and this renewal of the mind that someone transforms mean? To best understand what Paul is writing about, we need to look at the entirety of Romans 12:1-2.

"Therefore, I urge you, brothers and sisters, in view of God's mercy, to offer your bodies as a living sacrifice, holy and pleasing to God—this is your true and proper worship. Do not conform to the pattern of this world, but be transformed by the renewing of your mind. Then you will be able to test and approve what God's will is, His good, pleasing and perfect will."

God doesn't want us to get overtaken by the things that go on in this world; He wants us to seek Him and in all our ways honor Him. Proverbs 3:5-6 says, "Trust in the Lord with all your heart and lean not on your own understanding; in all your ways submit to Him, and He will make your paths straight."

When our minds line up with the will of God, we will begin to see and experience things differently. I seem to think sometimes people are afraid of being transformed into who God created them to be, thinking that they will lose something. So this brings upon transformation as the mind changes and your heart heals. Our minds and souls will thirst for change and something better.

Now that we are living in transformation from the old mindset and our old ways, now what?

Now we move on to the transformation. Paul is writing that when we live holy lives and present them to God each day, it is a form of worship. We should be so committed to living a holy life, and walking in a continual life of worship that we have no desire to fit into the world around us. Instead, we allow our minds to be consumed by God, His will, and what He tells us is good, acceptable and perfect. And, when our minds are filled with a focus on holiness, we will see and feel changed from the inside out-change in a manner where the world sees the difference, and God's way is seen as good and holy.

Yes, in this world, it may seem hard to remain focused on the ways of God and not the world around us. But when we do, we live not only an acceptable sacrifice to God, but also become a visible representation of Christ for the world to see. It is through our lives with Christ that the world can see and want to experience Christ, and the people in the world will witness the gospel in action. In our transformation, our great desire should be that people seek out God because their desire should also be to live like Jesus, and not like the world. Walking in a full transformation has benefits for you and it allows you to draw someone else to Jesus!

How do you know when you're going through spiritual transformation? It's a constant urge or pressing upon you to let go of parts of yourself and your life that are no longer a help to you. The Bible says in 2 Corinthians 5:17, "Therefore if any man be in Christ, he is a new creature: old things are passed away; behold, all things are become new."

Great transformations don't happen all at once and they can be difficult to identify, but after reflecting upon my own experiences and those of the people around me, I've been able to identify many of the signs indicating that transformation is indeed happening. Awareness is like road maps of understanding that can help you feel less alone while going through transition.

-Something feels off.

A feeling of something being off is something we all can relate to. Your job isn't fulfilling, but you don't know what else you want to do. Your relationship isn't satisfying, but you are afraid to be alone. You feel bored or passive, but you can't figure out how to get out of the rut.

These are the moments when we often start to blame and judge others because we don't want to take responsibility for our own fear and discontent we are going through at this moment. These feelings can become really overwhelming and depressing, and things can feel out of whack when caught up in our everyday lives. Although it's often scary or uncomfortable at first, being alone is one of the greatest gifts for acknowledging stagnation and understanding what's going on. Alone time helps reduce the clutter by having the extra space; it reduces distraction and cuts back on the things we used to cover up what's really wrong with us. Mediation also gives us a clear sense of what our distractions are. So, if you feel stuck, slow down, and spend some time alone. I'm not saying isolate yourself from everyone; just set aside some time to relax and think.

-It seems as if conflict is on every side!

Are you saying things you have never said to your parents or the people you love or care about? Maybe you have always thought about saying it, but held it in for the sake of peace. Are you fighting with your spouse, having a difficult time communicating with your children?

Sure, these could simply be the changes of life, but you can choose to look at it from a spiritual insight. If you are noticing a constant increase of conflict arising in different areas in your life, it's time to look deeper. If your life is pushing you toward changes, this is a good place to start. Rather than worry about the difficulties that are arising, simply try to become more aware. Write down what is happening, pay attention to how it makes you feel, and be open to why conflict is in all your relationships so you can help better yourself.

-You're rarely sleeping or sleeping all the time.

If you are feeling the blues of transformation, you might experience a small or a large amount of anxiety or depression. These feelings may encourage you to sleep all of the time or stop you from sleeping. The key to getting through it is simply to listen and respect your body. If you can't sleep, get up and read a book, write in a journal, or listen to music. If you're wiped out and need more sleep, set some time to build up your energy by taking a brisk walk or exercising- it helps your body produce positive energy! You know the old saying...you've got to make energy to have energy.

- Your emotions are out of control.

It feels exactly as it sounds. In the process of transformation, you can't contain your emotions. Tears well up in your eyes and sometimes roll down your face. Screams or moans come out of your mouth. You laugh or cry uncontrollably, and out of context. Don't try to bury these emotions or push these emotions aside. Allow the feelings to move through you, and you have to hope and stay in prayer before God; these things will pass. There is such strength in your emotions; a good scream will release all the negative energy that is going on down on the inside of you. So instead of taking your frustrations out on others, find time to scream or purchase you a punching bag to help redirect your emotions.

-You feel a sense of calm and inner peace.

When we have reached the peak of a real transformation, everything that doesn't matter seems to fall away. In that process of shedding off the old things, you become clear and calm and peaceful. Your body has less stress. And you are certain that things will work out exactly as God designed them to, because in reality, there really isn't any alternative but to trust in the Grace of God. As the Holy Spirit continues to guide you through life, I pray you have the strength to embrace the life God has created just for you.

Grace gives us boldness and confidence to trust God rather than trying to deal with life alone or fix our problems on our own. Walking in the Grace of God's strength allows us to go to Him with confidence every time there is a decision to make or a problem to fix. For out of His fullness (abundance), we have all received [all had a share and we were all supplied with] one grace after another and spiritual blessing upon spiritual blessing, and even favor upon favor and gift [heaped] upon gift. (John 1:16 AMPC). God's grace is supernatural! For by grace you have been saved through faith; and this is not of yourselves, it is the gift of God; not a result of works, so that no one may boast. (Ephesians 2:8-9 NASB)

What is divine grace? God's divine grace saves us, but it does so much more, in fact! It also sanctifies us and justifies us. Understanding God's divine grace and how it operates from His heart will help us better understand how to live by grace and walk in grace ourselves.

I SURVIVED, NOW WHAT?

Feeling like you're just fighting to keep your head above water or just to survive? Survival mode is real, and it stops us from living our best lives. Woman or Man of God, I see you. Even before your feet hit the floor, your heart is already overwhelmed with stress and worry. You have people pulling on you, needing your time, calling your name, wanting you to show up. If the truth be told, some days and some seasons are harder than others. Like me, you probably have experienced many sleepless nights, doctor appointments after doctor appointments, never-ending homework, crying children and changing hormones, and serious mood swings. It sounds crazy, but the struggle is real. You often find yourself wondering if you have anything left to give. A part of you questions even wanting to walk away or run away and hide from your daily responsibilities. Walk away from being needed; walk away to have quiet, to have peace. But you can't if you have a family depending on you. You do all you can to make it through the day. You get up. You push forward. You show up. You survive. If you are anything like me, survival mode will work you hard. You put that "I'm ok" face on so you can get through your day to get what's required of you done. You cook dinner. You do all you can to just make it to the next day, the next hour, the next minute, the next second. You've learned how to push on and keep going, even when you don't feel like it; or worse, don't want to get out the bed. Maybe you are at this place in your life; but please remember that surviving is not your stopping point. There is life beyond. I survive with the help and the grace of God; we can live full and prosperous lives.

TRUTH VS. HONESTY

The word honest isn't used as much as truth in the Bible. Honest means free of deceit and untruthfulness; sincere (you really believe it but what you are believing may not be true).

Truth is the quality or state of being true; that which is true or accordance of reality). Truth doesn't require any belief for it to be true.

What is belief? Belief is the acceptance that a statement is true, but it doesn't make the statement untrue if you don't believe it. Truth is most useful in the caterpillar stage. It's best to be truthful with yourself. You might think, "Why would I be lying to myself?" If we were to tell ourselves the truth, we lie to ourselves about a lot of stuff. But at some point, we have to face reality. An example would be if I apply for a job and I believe I'm the best person for the job, but the job hires someone else. To illustrate further, you might not have had a degree, or the other person might have had a better attitude. The other person probably could have worked longer hours and you couldn't. We blame others and refuse to take our part in the situation.

There are phases or levels to being truthful.

-Brutal Truth
This is just the plain truth!

-Polite Truth
This is co-signing or agreeing when you know you need to tell the person the truth instead of trying to spare their feelings.

-Honest Truth
This is the feeling of, "I honestly don't want to bother anyone today. I'm going through hell, but I won't bother you with it."

-Friendship/Relative Honesty
This is where one thinks, "Because of our relationship, I can't do it." But if you see a stranger disrespecting someone, you're quick to correct him or her. Yet when you see your friend or relative doing it, you do not correct them and you make excuses for them. We have got to be real and honest, no matter who it is.

Then Peter began to speak: "I now realize how true it is that God does not show favoritism but accepts from every nation the one who fears him and does what is right. (Acts 10:34-35 NIV)

Jesus said, "If you hold to my teaching, you are really My disciples. Then you will know the truth, and the truth will set you free." (John 8:31-32; John 8:36)

We have been taught that if we believe something that makes the statement true, but that's not the truth. We cannot create truth from our belief. Truth comes from facts. Jesus saith unto him, I am the way, the truth, and the life: no man cometh unto the Father, but by Me (John 14;6 KJV). Whether you believe it or not, it's the truth!

The truth is everlasting; it will not change. For example, two plus two equals four, and it will always be four.

BE WILLING TO TAKE ADVICE

Oftentimes, people don't take advice, even good advice. This is true even when the advice is free and when it's offered with love. Think about yourself. How often do you really, honestly take someone else's advice? How often do you say to yourself, or out loud, "That's a great idea. That's a much better way of doing it than the way I have been doing it." This type of meekness is almost unheard of in our society.

But think about the wisdom and knowledge God left here for us to follow. In order to grow, we need to see things differently. We don't want to keep doing the same things over and over if they're not working. Instead, we want our minds and spirits to open our eyes to new and better ways of doing things. But how can we see things differently if we refuse to take or accept Godly advice?

Sometimes, the reason we don't take advice is pure stubbornness. We want to do things our own way, even if it's not working! The way of a fool is right in his own eyes, but a wise man listens to advice. (Proverbs 12:15 ESV) The Bible also tells us, "Where there is no guidance, a people falls, but in an abundance of counselors there is safety. (Proverbs 11:14 ESV)

Other times, we avoid advice out of fear. We might be afraid we are going to look bad in the eyes of others, or we are going to feel useless. Or we might be fearful that the advice we get is not going to help. If we can't figure it out, then no one else can either. Maybe you have received bad advice or too much advice, then we promise ourselves never to make that mistake again.

Without counsel plans fail, but with many advisers they succeed. (Proverbs 15:22 ESV)

Listen to advice and accept instruction, that you may gain wisdom in the future. Many are the plans in the mind of a man, but it is the purpose of the Lord that will stand. (Proverbs 19:20-21)

I know when you have been hurt or misled in the advice area, it's hard to reach out again for advice. When you receive advice from others, use the Bible for your reference and if it lines up, take the advice. Life is so much simpler when you involve the strengths and wisdom of others. If we knew what to do to make our life better or more successful, we would already have done it. But if you're struggling in any aspect of your life (and we all do), we need advice. I'm convinced that one of the main reasons I've had some success in my life is my ability to receive wise and Godly counsel. I believe that if someone has worked hard, achieved some measure of success, and is willing to help, I'd be a fool not to listen!

If any of you lacks wisdom, you should ask God, who gives generously to all without finding fault, and it will be given to you. (James 1:5 NIV) By listening to someone and actually taking their advice, you not only get good results but you also get to contribute to the joy of another person.

Sometimes we can miss out on one of the main shortcuts to success, and that's being able to accept and receive advice from others. So often when a person struggles, he or she is very close to a breakthrough.

Rather than being content and grateful for what we have, we are focused on what's wrong with something and our need to fix it. When we are focused on what's wrong, it shows we are dissatisfied and discontent with our lives!

Whether it's related to ourselves, a disorganized closet, a scratch on the car, an imperfect accomplishment, a few pounds we would like to lose, or someone else's imperfections (the way someone looks, behaves, or lives his or her life) this very act of focusing on imperfections pulls us away from our goal of being kind and gentle to ourselves and others.

This way of thinking has nothing to do with trying to do your best, but being aware and focused on what's wrong with life. It's about realizing that it is always a better way to do something; this doesn't mean that you cannot enjoy and appreciate the way things already are.

This blueprint is to catch yourself when you fall into your old ways of thinking how things should be other than embracing what they are. It's good to remind yourself that life is okay the way it is, right now. Without your judgment, everything would be fine. As you begin to minimize your need for perfection in all areas of your life, you'll begin to look beyond the perfection or imperfection in life itself. We all know sometimes things happen beyond our control, but we have to handle every situation by accepting the truth in every situation.

LEARNING TO SAY NO-WHY DID I SAY YES?

Shift from survival mode to living according to the will of God and embracing your purpose-driven life. Don't be afraid to cut some things that don't benefit your day. Is it necessary? Nope. In some seasons, we must be willing to say no to things we want to do so we can have time for what God has assigned for us to do.

When cutting down your commitments, it is wise to seek God before agreeing to take an engagement. You need to pray for guidance in every area before you agree to say yes to a project or a speaking engagement. When praying concerning these things, ask yourself, "Why did I say yes? Was it out of obligation? Was it out of Fear? Am I people pleasing? Did I say yes to be seen? Whatever you do, be real with yourself. Why does this commitment matter? How much time does this project require? Will this project impact your family? Count up the cost. "Will I be responsible for this project? What happens if I say no?" These are just some things to pray about and meditate on to make sure when you say yes, it doesn't add stress to your life.

ALWAYS BE THANKFUL

One of the good things about being thankful is that the more you choose it, the easier it gets. The more you speak life to the things you already have, the more you notice you have a lot of things to be thankful for. Every time you start to complain or fuss about your day, take a moment to reflect on the good. Sometimes it is good to say what you are thankful about out loud: "I will praise thee, O Lord, with my whole heart; I will shew forth all thy marvelous works." (Psalm 9:1)

In this hour, we have to get up with a praise and go to bed with a praise, praising God for life and the things He has already graced us with. Being thankful is a daily choice, in spite of what we are going through. If we take the extra step and continue to remind ourselves, this will help the mind focus on the good things instead of the things we don't currently have. It's good to remind yourself how good God has been to you. "From the rising of the sun unto the going down of the same the Lord's name is to be praised." (Psalm 113:3)

The thief comes only to steal and kill and destroy; I have come that they may have life, and have it to the full. (John 10:10 NIV) Life and people will have a way of putting their hands around your neck and choking all your peace and joy right out of you. This will sometimes cause us to have a negative view of ourselves. We have to search or dig deep in ourselves to redevelop compassion for ourselves. It's not easy sometimes doing it on our own strength. We need the help of Jesus. We have to be willing to put in the work to take control of our thoughts.

Casting down imaginations, and every high thing that exalteth itself against the knowledge of God, and bringing into captivity every thought to the obedience of Christ; (2 Corinthians 10:5)

We deserve the same understanding, compassion, gentleness, and patience we so freely give to others. The type of understanding that says, "I know this hurts" and "How can I care for myself at this moment?" Instead of always being so hard on ourselves for all our shortcomings, self-compassion allows us to embrace our insecurities with kindness and understanding.

The next time you have an exhausting day and it seems like nothing you do goes or seems right, take a moment and give yourself some love. If you don't know where to start, here are a few things you can try.

FORGIVE YOURSELF.

Say this with me: "I forgive myself. "None of us are perfect, but we can strive to be what the Bible says: "Be ye therefore perfect, even as your Father which is in heaven is perfect." (Matthew 5:48 ES) We have all done things we are not proud of. Maybe you promised to spend more time with your children, but you watched television instead. Maybe you yelled at someone you loved just because you were tired. Maybe you said some hurtful things to a friend. Maybe you spent money you were supposed to save. I've been there. We have all probably laid awake at night thinking of all the ways we messed up. At times you can feel as if you mess up everything you put your hands and mind to. This is a lie from the enemy. Cast it down; the imagination only has power if you continue to let it run out of control. Bringing our thoughts into subjection to the word of Christ is the key to having mental freedom and control over your thoughts.

Sometimes the biggest obstacle in our way on the road to forgiveness is often the guilt that reminds us of our mistakes. This is a lie from the enemy. Guilt is meant to keep you bound-bound by your mistakes, and held in captivity by your thoughts. When we go to God and repent of our wrongdoings, we can lay our guilt and shame down. His word says, "If we confess our sins, He is faithful to and just to forgive us our sins and to cleanse us from all unrighteousness." (1John 1:9.) The next time you find yourself being hard on yourself, say out loud, "I forgive myself", then allow your heart to feel the forgiveness power of God's love to direct you on how to make the necessary changes without beating up on yourself.

PAST THE TEST THE FIRST TIME!

Have you ever asked yourself, "How many times do I have to repeat the same trial over again?"

I asked myself this when I seemed to be stuck in the same situation-feels like for the hundredth time. I cannot tell you how many times this one thorn in my flesh kept popping up in my life. When I began to seek God about why the situation kept coming back, I heard the Lord say clearly, "You keep falling for the same trick of the enemy; when obeying me concerning the situation, it will pass over." I would pray fast and cry out to God and it kept coming back after I was freed from the situation. I would have to cast the thoughts down and the thoughts would come right back. I would go through this over and over again until I learned to pass the test the first time; you would have thought I would have learned from the setback. But the most important pieces to moving forward is to learn the lesson the first time.

Setbacks can easily take you off course, or can reveal your true course. The difference between the distraction and the revelation is if you are willing to learn from your experience. When we allow ourselves to get caught up in the blame game, we learn NOTHING from our failures, often causing us to endure them AGAIN. Take time to step back and reflect on your failure. Why did it occur? Why is it still reoccurring? What parts were you responsible for? Was the situation outside your control? This process allowed me to have a good look at my situation so I would not repeat the same thing over again.

PREPARE FOR A COMEBACK!

Once you have learned from your experience and have reset your mindset, now you can prepare to plan your comeback. At this point, you have learned from your experience and you have changed your mindset. Are you ready for the comeback? Stepping out on faith and out of your comfort zone, it's time to put your failures behind you.

Not that I have already attained, or am already perfected; but I press on, that I may lay hold of that for which Christ Jesus has also laid hold of me. Brethren, I do not count myself to have apprehended; but one thing I do, forgetting those things which are behind and reaching forward to those things which are ahead, I press toward the goal for the prize of the upward call of God in Christ Jesus. (Philippians 3:12-14 NKJV)

God has given us the knowledge and the wisdom. You are confident and have the right resources to start a new beginning. I decree and declare now is the time to walk in the things and the places God has for you. Allow your LIFE to mirror your comeback. Your walk with Christ will show your confidence. Knowing God is with you should give you assurance to know who you are and what you are called to do.

Comebacks are sweeter. They remind us how far we have come, and give us joy knowing our setback didn't crush or kill us. You are very much alive. You were down temporarily, but you decided to rise to come above the water, knowing "When you pass through the waters, I will be with you; and when you pass through the rivers, they will not sweep over you. When you walk through the fire, you will not be burned; the flames will not set you ablaze". (Isaiah 43:2 NIV) It's time to keep moving! I believe in you!

SPIRITUAL REHAB

Rehabilitate-to restore (someone) to health or normal life by training and therapy after imprisonment, addiction, or illness. (Dictionary.com)

Now you have searched and explored all the unswept places-all the things you have buried deep down on the inside. You have put truth to all the lies you have told yourself. Now it's rehab time. It's time to reprogram your thinking with the biblical things of Christ. Thou wilt keep him in perfect peace, whose mind is stayed on thee: because he trusteth in thee. (Isaiah 26:3)

BINDING AND LOOSING

The word bind means to tie or fasten (something) tightly. This is exactly what you have to do with all the negative thoughts the enemy tries to bring back to your mind. You have got to be willing to put in the work if you want to stay in a place of peace.

Loose means to be free from confinement; not bound or tethered. Jesus tells us, "Verily I say unto you, whatsoever ye shall bind on earth shall be bound in heaven: and whatsoever ye shall loose on earth shall be loosed in heaven." (Matthew 18:18 KJV)

For example, when a thought comes to you saying "you will never succeed", begin to bind and loose the thought saying, "I bind this lie from the enemy and cast it back to the pit of hell and (loose).....I decree and declare I will succeed and I shall be prosperous, in Jesus's name." I'm not going to lie, you might have to do this a lot of times, but the key is to stay focused and keep your mind focused on Jesus!

Always be ready to war against any spirit that comes to your mind. The enemy will turn your very thoughts to imagination; you have to be ready to recognize the trick of the enemy and be ready to cast the thoughts down, "Casting down imaginations, and every high thing that exalteth itself against the knowledge of God, and bringing into captivity every thought to the obedience of Christ; And having in a readiness to revenge all disobedience, when your obedience is fulfilled.

Do ye look on things after the outward appearance? If any man trusts to himself that he is Christ's, let him of himself think this again, that, as he is Christ's, even so are we Christ's."
(2 Corinthians 10:5-7)

Even though the Bible tells us the Lord is married to the backslider (Jeremiah 3:14), this goes along with being rehabilitated. Walking in a renewed mind of the things Jesus has delivered us from will always come back to pull you back in; yet, you have to be mentally and physically ready to fight the enemy. Have you ever heard the saying, "if you play with fire, you will get burned?" If you begin to entertain the people or begin to revisit the places you have been delivered from, the enemy will pull you right back and you will find yourself back on that same merry-go-round just turning with no peace. Walking in a new place doesn't mean loneliness won't come; you just have to be ready to weather the storm. The Lord promised to be with us always; even when life doesn't seem fair (Matthew 28:20), Jesus promised to be with us.

I have always found it to be interesting that as long as we are crying and begging people to value us, they never seem to hear or see us. The second we give our lives to Christ, everything He delivered us from will offer us the world for a second chance to prove themselves. Let's see what the word of God has to say about this.

When the unclean spirit is gone out of a man, he walketh through dry places, seeking rest, and findeth none. Then he saith, "I will return into my house from whence I came out; and when he is come, he findeth it empty, swept, and garnished." Then goeth he, and taketh with himself seven other spirits more wicked than himself, and they enter in and dwell there: and the last state of that man is worse than the first. Even so shall it be also unto this wicked generation. (Matthew 12:43-45)

This simply means this person has searched for something better and could not find it; then when they see you with a sense of peace, they want to become a part of it. But in reality, they will add or bring seven times seven more problems than you had before-until you destroy them or they destroy you, whether in the natural or the spirit! Please don't look back; don't think back, and surely don't go back! It's an Illusion; please stay focused and keep moving in your new life.

DAILY PRAYER AND MEDITATION

At this point, we can agree that prayer and meditation will be a big help on your road to spiritual and emotional healing. Some people have never had a prayer life or spent time in mediation. Now is a good time to add at least one minute a day of prayer and meditation. You may laugh and say "One minute?", but remember, the more time you spend in prayer the longer you will find yourself praying and meditating. You are in a new place and new things take time to adjust to.

The key to making something a habit is to start small and simple, and stay consistent. Let's be real; if you've never meditated or spent time in prayer before, please do not try to commit to spending an hour in meditation every day. One minute a day is easier than making a one-hour commitment a day. Making unreasonable commitments from the start makes it more likely that you'll quit out of frustration too soon. We do not want to do anything that will cause you to be disappointed early on in your newfound spiritual walk with Christ.

Everyone handles stress differently; some of us overeat and gain weight, while others might stop eating and lose weight. If you take the time now to think about what habits you have when you are stressed, you can find new habits that will benefit you, and allow you to live longer. Maybe walking or reading a book, or working on a project that brings you a peace of mind can help reduce negative stress triggers. Whatever we do, we have to make sure that our new habits help you and not harm you. I like using the phrase, "One second, one minute, one hour, one day at a time". It helps me focus on the right now instead of tomorrow. Therefore, do not worry about tomorrow, for tomorrow will worry about itself. Each day has enough trouble of its own. (Matthew 6:34 NIV)

WHAT IF GOD SAID "NO?"

It is common for Christians to pray. In fact, one of the most important things a Christian can do in his or her life is pray. It is considered one of the "spiritual disciplines," which are ways we can talk to Jesus and help us grow closer to God.

For many of us, however, prayer is nothing more than asking God for things. We teach our children to recite simple prayers at meals or when they go to sleep. Athletes or coaches may send up a quick prayer before the big game. Pastors and small group leaders will open church meetings with prayer, inviting God to be present in the study or fellowship about to take place. And there are many for whom prayer is a sweet escape from the cares of the world to be alone with their Creator.

But when we pray, we ask God for things without taking the time to listen (listening will be addressed later). My question to you today is, how do you know God will answer your prayers? And what happens when God answers your most sincere prayer request with "no" or "wait"?

Many of us think that God will answer our prayers, regardless of what we ask for. We seem to think that's what He's there for, right?

We can very easily point to verses like John 14:13, which says, "Whatever you ask in My name, this I will do, that the Father may be glorified in the Son," and assume that this means that Jesus will always grant our requests. But this is not the case.

The truth of the matter is Jesus will say no. "For my thoughts are not your thoughts, neither are your ways my ways," declares the Lord. "As the heavens are higher than the earth, so are My ways higher than your ways and My thoughts than your thoughts. (Isaiah 55:8-9 NIV) God doesn't see things like we see them. He sees further down the road than we can. We have to learn to accept what He says.

First, we should look at what we are asking for. We may think that we are destined to have a certain thing, or to get a certain job, or to be married to a certain person. We have to stop and ask ourselves if what we are asking God for is right for us. Does it honor God? If we want a job just so we can earn more money, that may not be the right reason to take it; or a new relationship may pull you further away from God. Some prayers God will not say yes to-not to hurt us, but to bless us with something better.

It might be a good idea to look at the reason why we are asking for something: is it for self-gain or an even more sinful reason? When we ask for things that are clearly outside what God wants for us, this is a good reason for God to say no to our requests. Even if we do ask for good things but we just want God to give them to us because we think we deserve them, or think God owes us something, this motive is wrong also.

Finally, we should consider the divine will of God and His timing. God is working all things for our good (Romans 8:28), which means that He is working things out in our favor. There is no guarantee that what we are asking for will benefit us in the long run, or bring us closer to God if we got it.

Again, this is just a small window on why God answers or seems not to answer prayer. Again, no one can fully understand the heart and mind of God; Isaiah 55:8-9 says, "For My thoughts are not your thoughts, neither are your ways My ways, declares the LORD. For as the heavens are higher than the earth, so are My ways higher than your ways and My thoughts than your thoughts." This is just a guide for you to study if you want a better understanding of God's word.

WHEN GOD SAYS "YES"!

-God will confirm His word!

Whenever we want to know the will of God, we must always start with the word of God. When we are seeking the Lord's directions in our lives but we are not reading the Bible, it's like going on a road trip without directions.

What if we got in our cars to go on a vacation and just prayed that the Lord would help us find our way without any kind of written or computer instructions? This is what it is like when we ask for directions in our lives, but we ignore what God has already told us in the scriptures. "Study to shew thyself approved unto God, a workman that needeth not to be ashamed, rightly dividing the word of truth." (Timothy 2:15 KJV)

Through the word of God, we have been given a road map or a set of blueprints to guide or help us with important life decisions. Perhaps, an even better analogy than the road map is a great love letter. The word of God is like a letter from the Lord, Himself, meant to guide us forward into a glorifying life.

So when you desire to confirm that God really is saying "yes" to you, you must always consult the word of God to make sure you are not breaking any commands and to make sure you are headed in a Godly direction.

-God will open doors you need to walk through!

God will not say "yes" to you and then keep all the doors shut. When God is answering a prayer with a yes, He will confirm this word through the people, or maybe even circumstances in your life. For example, if God is saying "yes", that you should marry John, this will be confirmed by John also wanting to marry you. Or if you are asking that Tasha and you become engaged, Tasha taking the necessary steps to go forward with you will confirm this.

On the other hand, this could be one of the clearest signs He is giving you a "no" to the prayer you are asking. Sometimes people waste years of their lives trying to open doors God has closed and locked because they are not willing to accept no for an answer.

-He will give you peace in your heart.

The Bible says that God brings peace to those who follow Him. (Romans 5:1) When we begin to stray from God's will for our lives, one of the ways the Holy Spirit will lead us back onto the path He wants us on is by removing our peace. When you don't have peace about something, this could be God telling you not to move forward.

However, when God does tell you "yes," this will be confirmed by a genuine peace in your heart. You won't have to force it and you won't have to pretend to yourself that this is truly what God wants. You will know God is saying yes in your heart in such a way that you won't be able to explain it to others. 1 Corinthians 14:33 states, "For God is not a God of confusion, but of peace." Psalm 34:14 says, "Turn away from evil and do good; seek peace and pursue it."

We are told to pursue peace; therefore, God will lead you forward through showing you where the peace lies. By looking ahead and figuring out what choice brings you the most peace, you will then be able to confirm when God is saying "yes" to a decision you need to make.

-It will happen.

However, the one sign that will be the final confirmation that God really is saying "yes" is that the thing we are asking for will actually happen. God is not a man, that He should lie; neither the son of man, that He should repent: hath He said, and shall He not do it? Or hath He spoken, and shall He not make it good? (Numbers 23:19 KJV)

For I am the LORD: I will speak, and the word that I shall speak shall come to pass; it shall be no more prolonged: for in your days, O rebellious house, will I say the word, and will perform it, saith the Lord GOD. (Ezekiel 12:25 KJV)

LISTENING

He who has ears to hear, let him hear. (Matthew 11:15) God speaks to all of us; we have to be willing to hear what He has to say. We have to position ourselves to hear God. I'm sure we have all heard God speak to us. Have you ever been driving down the road and a voice says, "Turn right", and for some strange reason, you turn right; then you hear later that a really bad accident was on your original route and you take that deep breath saying, "Thank you Jesus." God has a way of speaking to us; we just have to be willing to listen and obey.

Now imagine if we have a daily communication and prayer life with Christ. We will be able to recognize and know His voice. My sheep hear my voice, and I know them, and they follow Me:
And I give unto them eternal life; and they shall never perish, neither shall any man pluck them out of My hand. (John 10:27-28 KJV).

Once we begin to follow the voice of Christ (Bible), we will become more in tune to the voice of God. To tell the truth, God has always had a plan from the very beginning; when He created this world, He had a plan. For day and night, heavens and earth, land and sea, sun and moon, birds and fish, animals and humans-He has always had a plan. And just four verses into His Word, we can see that He likes His plan. He calls it good. Towards the end of creation, He calls His plan very good (study Genesis 1).

God's plan is good because of the purpose it will serve. It is good because of the hope it will give. It is good because of the lives it will save. But really, it is good simply because God says it's good.

Yes, God still has plans for you. He knew the span of your life before you were formed in your mother's womb.(Jeremiah 1:5) He knows the hairs on your head (Luke 12:7), the thoughts in your mind (Psalm 94:11), and the hours that you will live on this earth (Psalm 139:16). He would not leave such attention to detail merely to chance. God has plans for you, and they are good. (Jeremiah 29:11)

It's no good having a plan if we don't follow it. Our actions betray our intentions. Sometimes our choices follow our own desires, rather than God's. In life, we will have many choices to make each and every day. If we choose not to listen carefully to the Lord in every area, it puts us in danger of going in the wrong direction to Him, and we end up far from where we should be.

MOVING PAST THE GUILT

Guilt refers to the unpleasant feeling of regret stemming from the belief that you could or should have done something different at the time a traumatic event occurred-maybe when a person decides to walk away from a toxic relationship, job, or place but suffers from overwhelming guilt and grief. If we confess our sins, He is faithful and just to forgive us our sins, and to cleanse us from all unrighteousness. (1John 1:9)

I have realized sometimes, people are unable to find that feeling of reconciliation or peace with God. No matter how often they confess, and after doing all that they can to make amends for their sin, they still feel as if they cannot be forgiven. It may seem like their sins or issues like divorce, abortion, or adultery are beyond God's forgiveness. They continue to carry the burden of their guilt along with them each day, weighed down by a feeling of permanent distance in their relationship with the Lord.

Perhaps the spirit of guilt has overtaken you, and you feel like you are sinking in sorrow and regret. What is preventing you from moving beyond your past and feeling forgiven? I found it to be true that some people lie to themselves; but how are you going to overcome guilt if you won't tell yourself the truth? Ask yourself why it is a need to hold on to this lie. Does it satisfy you somehow? Let's deal with these issues so we can mentally lay the feelings of guilt on the altar.

Jesus said, "Come to me, all you who are weary and burdened, and I will give you rest. Take my yoke upon you and learn from me, for I am gentle and humble in heart, and you will find rest for your souls. For my yoke is easy and my burden is light." (Matthew 11:28-30 NIV) The more you pray, the more you will be able to expose and cast down every negative thought or negative feeling from the enemy. The Bible tells us to have nothing to do with the fruitless deeds of darkness, but rather expose them. It is shameful even to mention what the disobedient do in secret. (Ephesians 5:11-12 NIV)

In order for our minds to be free, let's expose the enemy before God. You might say, "What does that mean?" It means to tell God all about it. Jesus tells us to "Come to me, all you who are weary and burdened, and I will give you rest. (Matthew 11:28 NIV)

In order for the mind to rest, we have to learn to cast our burdens upon the Lord. This means to simply trust Him. It's hard to even trust God after people have disappointed you. This is why the Bible says, "No one can serve two masters. Either you will hate the one and love the other, or you will be devoted to the one and despise the other. You cannot serve both God and money." This can also mean people as well.

Thou wilt keep him in perfect peace, whose mind is stayed on thee: because he trusteth in thee. (Isaiah 26:3 kJV)

We can sometimes think, "Because I am still suffering the effects from my sin, God must not have forgiven me yet." It is easy to confuse natural consequences with God's punishment; however, they are different. If you jump from a balcony, you might have sprained your ankle. God did not cause your ankle to twist to punish you. The fact that you made a decision to jump from the balcony caused you to hurt your ankle. Your pain is simply a consequence of your action.

In the same way, sins for which we have been forgiven long ago may still have consequences in our lives. An ex-spouse may be difficult to get along with. We may grieve on the due date of the baby that was aborted. We may suffer injuries from the accident that occurred while we were drinking. Yet, none of these troubles represents God's punishment.

According to Romans 5:9-10, God saves us from His wrath: Since we have now been justified by His blood, how much more shall we be saved from God's wrath through Him! For if, when we were God's enemies, we were reconciled to Him through the death of His Son, how much more, having been reconciled, shall we be saved through His life! (NIV) Our punishment has been paid in Christ.

As believers, we are forgiven for our actions and precious to the Lord, even when consequences from those actions remain in our lives. I found it to be true that if you want to be free from tormenting thoughts, you are going to have to pray, fast, worship and praise your way through guilt. You can be free and there is life after the pain, and it's called freedom and joy.

EMOTIONAL BALANCE

Emotional balance is a state of being aware of your emotions enough to manage them in a way that is understanding, honest, and wise. It's important to be aware of your emotions. Emotional balance can also be defined as having dealt with the highs and lows, good and bad, success or failure in your own life.

Examples are:
Apologies - being able to admit and apologize for what you have done.
Restitution - having recognized and paid back a debt that you owed to a friend or a loved one in order to restore peace.

Forgiveness and self-forgiveness - being able to forgive the person who has offended you and having forgiven yourself for allowing it to happen.

If you have not done these things, you need to:
-Stop lying to yourself.
-Seek professional therapy from your Pastor or a professional Counselor.

-See a medical doctor to help get balance. (It's ok if you need the help; please go get it!)

Talking +Understanding +Action

Talking is important, but no amount of talking will work on its own. Talking must be followed by action. It's important to understand that action has to be required along with talking. As the body without the spirit is dead, so faith without deeds is dead. (James 2:26)

-Communication
-Talking
-Listening
-Understanding

These components have to work as one. Talking by itself is just rambling. What's rambling? Rambling is just one-sided communication, sort of like being selfish. When you pray, don't ramble like heathens who think they'll be heard if they talk a lot. (Matthew 6:7 GWT 1995)

If God requires us not to ramble, how do we expect people to understand us when we ramble? We as people do not want to listen, but always want to express ourselves or always want others to listen to us-it goes back to being (selfish). We need to train ourselves to listen instead of talking all the time. Understand this, my dear brothers and sisters: You must all be quick to listen, slow to speak, and slow to get angry. (James 1:19 NLT)

We will save ourselves a lot of emotional issues if we learn to listen. Not listening is a waste of time in so many ways. One thing we can all agree on is time is one thing we cannot get back.

To illustrate, we waste the Counselor, the Pastor, the Doctor's time if we don't want real help. If we want someone to vent to, even the person doing the listening will get tired and begin rescheduling appointments. Your friends will stop answering the phone because they know you are not ready to let go of the thing that causes you so much emotional stress. If we cannot find peace in the lives we choose to live in, it's time to take action in order to find the necessary peace that's needed so we can find real emotional balance.

Action is going to get the help you need or making changes, while intention is acknowledging you need help. Intention is not a solution-if you really don't go get the help (or even worse, you don't want the help). It's something to think about. It sounds harsh when the word tells us, "So Jesus said to the Jews who had believed him, 'If you abide in My word, you are truly My disciples, and you will know the truth, and the truth will set you free'." (John 8:31-32 ESV)

There are those who hate the one who upholds justice in court and detest the one who tells the truth. (Amos 5:10 NIV) We've got to find a way to break unhealthy emotions. I really do believe if we are willing to admit that we have an unhealthy emotional balance, we can then begin to make the necessary changes we need to be a better person. Having emotional balance helps us to gain flexibility and stabilization and build a bridge between our minds and bodies. In other words, emotional balance teaches us how to respond to negative emotions and thoughts without just getting stuck in them.

Some signs of an unhealthy emotional balance are:

-Anger, irritability, or restlessness.
-Feeling overwhelmed, unmotivated, or unfocused.
-Trouble sleeping or sleeping too much.
-Racing thoughts or constant worry.
-Problems with your memory or concentration.
-Making bad decisions.
-Depression or anxiety.

If you are experiencing more than one, it is a good idea to seek help.

Sometimes as people, we might think we don't have the ability to change. Today is March 3, 2021; prior to this day, my friend John, would tell me, "Tina, your personality is too masculine. I have been married, and at this point in my life, I'm divorced. Neither husband wanted a divorce, but neither wanted to be married either; so for my sanity's sake, I left. It will be easy for me to point fingers or bash them, but it has now or never been about them; it has always been about me. I have been independent for so long until it's commonplace for me to do things on my own. If the sink is leaking and I bring it to the attention of the head of the household, and two weeks later it's not done, that irritates my last nerve! So I'd call the plumber to have it fixed. When it's fixed, it's a "you didn't give me time" kind of situation; yet, it had been weeks with no results when I reminded them I was going to get it done. So being me, I just did it and I found that to be a problem.

Learning how to sit back and allow someone to lead was hard for me because I was raised to be a leader. Let me add, I grew up in a two-parent home until my dad passed away. I always watched my mom submit, but my dad let her handle all the money because he was freehearted. He would have given it all away, and I watched my mom submit. Yet my dad taught me to be independent as well; so all I knew how to do was lead and not follow. I was having a quiet moment and I heard, "You have to want to want to change. Change is not hard; it has to be something you are willing and ready to do. Nothing just happens by chance." We have to be willing to put ourselves in other people's shoes and be willing to make healthy decisions.

-Communication
-Talking
-Listening
-Understanding

It will even work when we sit down and soul search ourselves. The Bible says, "Anyone with ears to hear should listen and understand!" (Matthew 11:15 NLT)

Sometimes it's hard to receive the truth when others are trying to communicate how they feel. When we feel threatened, things can go left quickly, and that's when the unhealthy communication begins. Whoever loves discipline loves knowledge, but whoever hates correction is stupid. (Proverbs 12:1 NIV)

At all times, we need to have a correctable spirit. Whoever ignores instruction despises himself, but he who listens to reproof gains intelligence. (Proverbs 15:32) We should always have a spirit or mindset where we can be taught something. For whoever has [a teachable heart], to him more [understanding] will be given; and whoever does not have [a yearning for truth], even what he has will be taken away from him." (Mark 4:25 Amplified Bible)

LISTENING AND UNDERSTANDING

Listen to understand instead of thinking about what you want to say while the other person is talking; really listen to them. People often call this "active listening". A few things to pay attention to when someone is talking to you include:

-Pay attention.

When someone is talking to you, look at them. Keep eye contact and pay attention to what their body language is saying.

-Don't interrupt.

The best way to make someone feel like they are not being ignored is to not to interrupt or talk on top of them. Listen and wait until they are done to ask questions or add your thoughts. Sometimes when the conversation is deep or the feelings are high, this might be hard to do. Listening without angry or ill feelings helps the conversation to go better.

-Respond to what they said.

Take a few seconds to breath. Remember to be honest and respectful in your responses, and remember to talk and listen in a way you want to be talked to. Most importantly, listen in a way you want to be listened to.

Listening is a very important skill you can have. How well you listen might have a major impact on your job success, and having healthy relationships with others.

We listen to get information.
We listen to understand.
We listen for pleasure, entertainment & relaxation.
We listen to learn.

In our lives, we do a lot of listening. Improving our listening skills can be beneficial. Becoming a better listener can improve productivity, as well as the ability to influence and negotiate. Listening will also minimize and help avoid conflict and misunderstandings.

SELF-AWARENESS

Throughout this book, I have talked about self-awareness in many different ways.

Self-awareness gives us a better understanding of ourselves. We are able to experience ourselves as unique individuals. We are then empowered to make changes and to build and strengthen areas of our lives that need strengthening, as well as identify areas where we would like to make improvements.

What happens if we can't or refuse to make changes to ourselves for the better? Let's look at the caterpillar again. If the caterpillar is unable to transition, at this point, the caterpillar will continue to feed while there is food available until it can no longer grow. Eventually, feeding slows down and eventually stops. Since the caterpillar does not form a cocoon or pupa, it eventually dies from dehydration. To better understand, the chrysalis (cocoon) protects the caterpillar as it begins to turn itself into liquid; the caterpillar's body has to go through this stage so it can transform. If it's unable to do so, it dies.

Dehydration occurs in the human body when more water and fluids leave the body than enters it. Even low levels of dehydration can cause headaches, lethargy, and constipation. The human body is roughly 75 percent water. Without this water, it cannot survive. (Dictionary.com)

Wow...it dies from dehydration. Let's look at this in a spiritual sense and see how it affects us in a natural sense. The Bible tells us, "Do not conform to the pattern of this world, but be transformed by the renewing of your mind. Then you will be able to test and approve what God's will is--his good, pleasing and perfect will."(Romans 12:2 NIV)

If we don't allow ourselves to be transformed to a better mindset, it will affect many areas in our lives. It will affect your relationship with people, such as the people you work with, your husband, kids, and if you are reading this and can't seem to build healthy relationships, it's something about you that needs to be transformed. Rather, it's your attitude or it's the way you perceive things. You might be a complainer who complains about everything and never can seem to be thankful for anything. You might be controlling, and want to control every situation without compromising. Life will not always be about you! We have to live in a changing world and know when to speak, when to hold on, when to let go and when to simply keep moving. So you see, not being able to change hurts is in so many ways.

Self-awareness is so important. It helps us to be better people and it helps us to build healthy relationships with the people around us. "For to be carnally minded is death; but to be spiritually minded is life and peace." (Romans 8:6 KJV) "For the mind that is set on the flesh is hostile to God, for it does not submit to God's law; indeed, it cannot. Those who are in the flesh cannot please God." (Romans 8:7-8 NIV)

Now this is interesting! This verse doesn't even present this as a command, but as a simple statement of fact (the verb in verse five is in the indicative mood, not the imperative; it's not a command, it's a reality). However, the command is found in this text.

"If, then, you have been raised with Christ, seek the things that are above, where Christ is, seated at the right hand of God. Set your minds on things that are above, not on things that are on earth." (Colossians 3:1-2 NIV)

Developing a spiritual mindset is clearly something we must do. So a spiritual mindset is not only a reality, but also an evidence of your spiritual condition. It is also a responsibility. Setting your mind on spiritual things is a command to be obeyed.

"When you were slaves to sin, you were free from the control of righteousness. What benefit did you reap at that time from the things you are now ashamed of? Those things result in death! But now that you have been set free from sin and have become slaves of God, the benefit you reap leads to holiness, and the result is eternal life." (Romans 6:20-22 NIV)

Whether we want to believe it or not, sinner or saint, we are going to be a slave to something. Either it benefits us, or causes us some type of emotional or physical pain. "Don't you know that when you offer yourselves to someone as obedient slaves, you are slaves of the one you obey--whether you are slaves to sin, which leads to death, or to obedience, which leads to righteousness?" (Romans 6:16 NIV)

WAYS YOU CAN RECOGNIZE YOUR HEALING

-You know yourself much better.

Hopefully, you have used the pain you have gone through in your life to learn about yourself and grow, leaving you in a much better place to build healthy memories and relationships.

-You are able to embrace the good and bad of your past.

When you have moved along to the path of healing, you will start to notice that you can acknowledge and accept both the good and bad aspects of your past. You now have a much more realistic view and it is genuine; so it feels better to you.

-The ups and downs are less severe.

Healing is a process with good days and bad days. At the beginning, the difference between those good and bad days can be a mess. One day, you will only think about your past 10 times, but refrain from texting and calling people to tell them off or remind them of how they hurt you. The next day, you might not want to get out of bed, due to overwhelming feelings of sadness and anger, and an uncontrollable urge to reach out to the people who hurt you.

It is hard to imagine when you are in the middle of this, but gradually, those shifts start to smooth out and you find yourself in a more comfortable place that feels good and the thoughts have faded away.

-You have more of an understanding of why the situation happened.

Making sense of a painful experience is one of the keys to healing. We often know what incident or what that final straw was that made us walk away. Truly understanding the relationship/friendship motion and our own part in how it went down is very empowering, and can lead you to being at peace with the outcome. It also gives you important information about yourself to take into your next relationship/friendship.

-You're getting better at naming your feelings.

When you are angry, disappointed or hurt, you are better at expressing those feelings in a way that helps you better cope and helps how you treat others when you are not having a good day.

-When things go wrong, you don't automatically blame yourself.

Self-blame and self-criticism are the worst habits or mistakes we can learn. Sometimes, self-blame can be a constant echo of what you have been told repeatedly. When we are able to look at our failures and mistakes in a more complex way and acknowledge the roles of others, your own role, as well as other factors, is most definitely a sign of progress.

-You are gaining self-confidence.

You have moved past second-guessing yourself. This can be a good seed if you keep watering and nurturing it until it actually begins to grow; self-confidence is the key to breaking those old depressing negative thoughts running through your head in the middle of night-the ones that challenge your every decision, and make you wonder if you will ever do anything right.

-You're able to speak up for yourself in a positive manner.

You're now speaking up for yourself in a positive manner without worrying about what other people think or feel. When we learn people's roles in our lives, it's easier to handle sensitivity and rejection. Being aware of people's thoughts and where you stand in their lives makes situations a lot easier to deal with and keeps things moving forward.

-You respect boundaries and set your own.

You have gained the ability to recognize healthy boundaries. Boundaries of others and your own are most definitely a sign of your ability to connect in healthier ways. As you begin to see yourself in fullness, it becomes easier to see others in the same way. You take pride in what you handled well and coped with what you blocked out.

-You congratulate yourself and celebrate your progress.

Your ability to congratulate yourself and celebrate your progress, as well as deal with mistakes and failures, is another way to measure how far you have come in your healing process. Having self-compassion, especially when you mess up, is a very important part of growth and self-compassion, although it is usually slow in coming. That old place where you would beat yourself up mentally and emotionally is no longer a problem.

-You are more accepting of your appearance.

Accepting yourself and the way you look is a game changer. As you begin to let go of some of the negativity people have placed upon you about the way you look and your physical appearance, the happier you will be. Your appearance will change for the better the more you believe in yourself and take care of yourself.

-You are no longer ashamed.

If you are married or single, you accept your status. The shame of being unloved, or feeling singled out in this way, and the need to be isolated from others slowly begin to fade away as you come into your own understanding of yourself. Understanding that you are not alone and that many others face a similar battle helps you overcome the shame that was never yours to begin with. We have to live our own lives and not the image we see of others. Being different feels pretty good.

-You are now setting personal goals.

This is actually a very big deal because the broken you often felt a sense of hopelessness, especially when it comes to personal growth; the chances are good that you have recognized what was said to you and about you, whether in childhood or adulthood. It no longer defines you or limits your ability to succeed; spoken words no longer control you. You have recognized spoken words are just spoken words.

Healing can sometimes be a long and slow process. We have to be thankful for even the smallest sign of progress when there are signs of change and growth along the way. Remember to be your own cheerleader and to practice self-compassion when the old you start to come back up. Remember you are worthy!

-Your change is beginning to show.

You find yourself singing a different song out loud. You no longer want to listen to that song that is associated with your situation. This is a great sign that you have changed to your butterfly form. Just keep singing your new song. Things that used to scare you don't anymore. You may find yourself driving to places that you were afraid to go alone. You might be thinking about changing careers-doing something you love-instead of just working to have a job. You might also find yourself standing up to people who may have intimidated you in the past. These are all signs of inner strength and emotional healing.

You are ready to make some big changes to your living situation. You may want to move or remodel the house. It may be that you associated your surroundings to when you were feeling bad, so wanting to change them is a way of telling yourself that you are ready to feel good again. I would try moving some furniture around or taking a trip, however, before putting the house on the market; (smile) one step at a time.

You understand that bad days are only temporary. We all have bad days, but for someone who has been going through a hard time, the thoughts of a setback are not far away. Yet in this second, in this minute, in this hour, you are enjoying the moment and allowing tomorrow to take care of itself.

You have more moments of peace and you are sleeping better. This is another sign that your mood has gotten better. You are starting to recognize those peaceful moments and if you were waking up with anxiety and you are doing this less often, you are moving in the right direction. Peace is a beautiful thing; learn to enjoy the moment.

As you continue to heal, you will also grow as a person and your relationships will deepen, even though the enemy will try to bring those old thoughts back to you. Don't allow the enemy to do that to you. Stand fast on the word of God and hold on to the promises God has graced you with.

THE DEATH OF LAZARUS

1. Now a man named Lazarus was sick. He was from Bethany,
the village of Mary and her sister Martha.

2. (This Mary, whose brother Lazarus now lay sick, was the same one who poured perfume on the Lord and wiped his feet with her hair.)
3. So the sisters sent word to Jesus, "Lord, the one you love is sick."
4. When He heard this, Jesus said, "This sickness will not end in death. No, it is for God's glory so that God's Son may be glorified through it."
5. Now Jesus loved Martha and her sister and Lazarus.
6. So when He heard that Lazarus was sick, He stayed where He was two more days,
7. and then He said to His disciples, "Let us go back to Judea."
8. "But Rabbi," they said, "a short while ago the Jews there tried to stone you, and yet you are going back?"
9. Jesus answered, "Are there not twelve hours of daylight? Anyone who walks in the daytime will not stumble, for they see by this world's light.
10. It is when a person walks at night that they stumble, for they have no light."
11. After He had said this, He went on to tell them, "Our friend Lazarus has fallen asleep; but I am going there to wake him up."
12. His disciples replied, "Lord, if he sleeps, he will get better."
13. Jesus had been speaking of his death, but His disciples thought He meant natural sleep.
14. So then He told them plainly, "Lazarus is dead,
15. and for your sake I am glad I was not there, so that you may believe. But let us go to him."
16. Then Thomas (also known as Didymus) said to the rest of the disciples, "Let us also go, that we may die with him."

JESUS COMFORTS THE SISTERS OF LAZARUS

17. On His arrival, Jesus found that Lazarus had already been in the tomb for four days.
18. Now Bethany was less than two miles from Jerusalem,
19. and many Jews had come to Martha and Mary to comfort them in the loss of their brother.
20. When Martha heard that Jesus was coming, she went out to meet Him, but Mary stayed at home.
21. "Lord," Martha said to Jesus, "if You had been here, my brother would not have died.
22. But I know that even now God will give You whatever you ask."
23. Jesus said to her, "Your brother will rise again."

24. Martha answered, "I know he will rise again in the resurrection at the last day."

25. Jesus said to her, "I am the resurrection and the life. The one who believes in Me will live, even though they die;

26. and whoever lives by believing in Me will never die. Do you believe this?"

27. "Yes, Lord," she replied, "I believe that You are the Messiah, the Son of God, who is to come into the world."

28. After she had said this, she went back and called her sister Mary aside. "The Teacher is here," she said, "and is asking for you."

29. When Mary heard this, she got up quickly and went to Him.

30. Now Jesus had not yet entered the village, but was still at the place where Martha had met Him.

31. When the Jews who had been with Mary in the house, comforting her, noticed how quickly she got up and went out, they followed her, supposing she was going to the tomb to mourn there.

32. When Mary reached the place where Jesus was and saw Him, she fell at His feet and said, "Lord, if You had been here, my brother would not have died."

33. When Jesus saw her weeping, and the Jews who had come along with her also weeping, He was deeply moved in spirit and troubled.

34. "Where have you laid him?" He asked. "Come and see, Lord," they replied.

35. Jesus wept.

36. Then the Jews said, "See how He loved him!"

37. But some of them said, "Could not He who opened the eyes of the blind man have kept this man from dying?"

JESUS RAISES LAZARUS FROM THE DEAD

38. Jesus, once more deeply moved, came to the tomb. It was a cave with a stone laid across the entrance.

39. "Take away the stone," He said.

"But, Lord," said Martha, the sister of the dead man, "by this time there is a bad odor, for he has been there four days."

40. Then Jesus said, "Did I not tell you that if you believe, you will see the glory of God?"

41. So they took away the stone. Then Jesus looked up and said, "Father, I thank You that You have heard Me.

42. I knew that You always hear Me, but I said this for the benefit of the people standing here, that they may believe that You sent me."
43. When He had said this, Jesus called in a loud voice, "Lazarus, come out!"
44. The dead man came out, his hands and feet wrapped with strips of linen, and a cloth around his face. Jesus said to them, "Take off the grave clothes and let him go." (John 11:1-44 NIV)

This passage has been on my mind and in my spirit for almost a year. This passage has several statements I would like to shed some light on. Lazarus's story is a good example of transformation. Lazarus's sisters, Mary and Martha, sent a message to Jesus saying their brother, whom Jesus loved, was sick.

When Jesus received the message, He stated this sickness will not end in death. Jesus was not in a hurry to get back to Judea, so He stayed where He was for two more days.

Jesus had His own issues going on in Judea; we learned this from His conversation with His disciples. Yet, Jesus began His trip back to Judea to see about His friend, Lazarus, whom He loved.

On the trip back Jesus said, "Our friend Lazarus has fallen asleep; but I am going there to wake him up." His disciples replied, "Lord, if he sleeps, he will get better." Jesus had been speaking of his death, but his disciples thought he meant natural sleep.

One can say, "Well, if Jesus loved him, why did it take him two days to go see about him?" We can even use this in our lives; when trials and tribulations come, we feel forsaken. The Bible says we can rejoice, too, when we run into problems and trials, for we know that they help us develop endurance. (Romans 5:3 NLT)

The disciples didn't understand, so Jesus said, "Lazarus is dead and for your sake, I am glad I was not there, so that you may believe. But let us go to him." Jesus knew Lazarus would already be dead because He told His disciples God would be glorified in Lazarus's situation. When Jesus arrived in Judea, Martha heard that He was coming. She went out to meet Him, but Mary stayed at home. "Lord," Martha said to Jesus, "if You had been here, my brother would not have died."

Let's look at this in another sense besides a natural death. We can even use this in our lives; when trials and tribulations come we feel forsaken. We feel if Jesus really loved us, we wouldn't be having such a hard time. In all our situations, it's a time and a season for Jesus to work on our situation. For example, Lazarus's sisters had seen the wonderful miracles of Jesus, yet she blamed Him for not being present to help Lazarus. Even now, some of us feel the way Martha felt.

Jesus promised to always be with us. Just because we hit hard times doesn't mean God is not present. God is our refuge and strength, always ready to help in times of trouble. (Psalm 46:1)
We just have to be patient and wait until our appointed time to come out of whatever it is we are going through.

Jesus asked Martha, "Do you believe?" In other words, He was saying where is your faith?

Even when Mary reached the place where Jesus was, she fell to the feet of Jesus in an emotional rant crying in her own way, blaming Jesus for her brother's situation. Jesus saw and felt the hurt and He began to cry also. We have to understand that Jesus loves us. I believe as He sits on the throne, He intercedes to His Father with this same type of passion the Bible shows us He had towards Martha, Mary and Lazarus.

Jesus said to them to take away the stone. Just like He is saying to us, "Allow me to take away the hurt, the pain, the shame the disappointment in life. Are we being like Martha, giving Him an excuse, or are we gonna believe the words He told Martha: "Did I not tell you that if you believe, you will see the glory of God?" So they obeyed and took away the stone. Now after reading all of this, are you ready to take away your stone?

Jesus looked up and said, "Father, I thank You that You have heard Me. I knew that You always hear Me, but I said this for the benefit of the people standing here, that they may believe that You sent me." When He had said this, Jesus called in a loud voice, "Lazarus, come out!" The dead man came out, his hands and feet wrapped with strips of linen, and a cloth around his face. Jesus said to them, "Take off the grave clothes and let him go."

Men and women of God! God is calling us up and out of depression and our sins so He can heal us; yet, we have to be willing to surrender the stone to Him. I believe that it's an appointed time to be healed and delivered. What I love about Jesus is He is not going to force His way in. He asks us to confess with our mouths and believe with our hearts He is the Messiah, and believe that He is ready, able and willing to remove the stones that have us bound. The question again is will you allow Him to? The word stone for me means problems, sickness or issues that weigh us down. Jesus wants to heal us so our lives and our stories can draw others to Christ so His divine healing power can be shown through us.

I was up mediating this morning (March 12, 2021), and I began to think about how God healed my broken heart. God used love. For God so loved the world, that He gave His only begotten Son, that whosoever believeth in Him should not perish, but have everlasting life. (John 3:16)

He used Godly men to help guide me through my caterpillar season. The very thing that broke me, He turned around and used the same thing to help heal me. I think of the scripture 1 Corinthians 13. When people come into our lives, they come for a reason, a time and a season. We can misread that season if we are in the flesh, thinking God sent them for one reason. We can get our emotions all tied and tangled up in them and destroy the purpose or the reason God sent them.

To illustrate, if I'm a single woman and God sent a single man, my thoughts might be, "Oh, maybe he is my husband", and from there things go left when in fact, God sent him so His (God) love can be exemplified for the up building of His kingdom, bringing others to Christ.

When I think of the wonderful and unexplainable love of Jesus, I think of, "Though the mountains be shaken and the hills be removed, yet My unfailing love for you will not be shaken nor My covenant of peace be removed," says the Lord, who has compassion on you. (Isaiah 54:10 NIV)

My caterpillar experience taught me that being married, sex, money or things, traveling from place to place could not heal me; LOVE could and did. I met my best friend some time ago and we became friends. At the time, he had not been to church in over ten years. It was two people from different walks of life. God used us to teach each other the power of God's love. He lives in one city and I live in another; yet we talk everyday. I was hurting, broken and scarred from life, and so was he in a sense. My life showed that all ministers and women were not the same and his life showed me the same. His caterpillar experiences were different from mine, but we were able to learn from each other's experience, thoughts and views, and achieve an answer from the word of God-the Bible.

I am convinced that with everything we experience in this life, we can find an answer in the Bible. What has been will be again, what has been done will be done again; there is nothing new under the sun. (Ecclesiastes 1:9 NIV) We can all have the butterfly experience. I don't care who you were or what you have done; I do know, "But He was wounded for our transgressions, He was bruised for our iniquities: the chastisement of our peace was upon Him; and with His stripes we are healed." (Isaiah 53:5 KJV)

TRIGGERS

An emotional trigger is anything-including memories, experiences, or events-that trigger an intense emotional reaction, regardless of your current mood. Emotional triggers can also be linked to post-traumatic stress disorder (PTSD). (dictionary.com)

I was having a conversation with a friend and we were talking about something (I can't remember the whole conversation); but somehow, we started talking about relationships. Out of nowhere, I went off on a rant for about five minutes; my friend didn't say anything and just allowed me to finish. All of a sudden, I became quiet because I was trying to figure out to myself what in the world was going on, and what had set me off into a frantic rant. I heard him say, "You just had a trigger and you snapped for about five minutes!" (LOL!) Y'all, he is petty! I believe he timed me just to be specific. He loves facts. In a steady voice he said, "You need therapy!" I couldn't disagree because I was trying to figure out where it came from. I honestly don't have anything in my heart against the person. I found out I was disappointed because God allowed me to go through it.

My friend asked, "What made you so important that you can't go through something? We all go through things; we just have to be thankful we made it through and didn't die in it." So even in your butterfly stage, some of your caterpillar experiences will show up. It's up to us to deal with it and why it showed up. It's time to fast and pray so you can filter your spirit of these negative emotions. Sometimes when people hear "you need to see a therapist", they flip. But it will help you move on to the next phase of your life. Closure is not a bad thing; even if that person never apologizes, you can make peace with yourself so you can continue your journey of drawing people to a loving and wonderful God!

SOME THINGS THAT MIGHT CAUSE THE TRIGGERS

• the anniversary dates of losses or trauma
• frightening news events
• too much to do, feeling overwhelmed
• family friction
• the end of a relationship
• spending too much time alone
• being judged, criticized, teased, or put down
• financial problems, getting a big bill
• physical illness
• sexual harassment
• being yelled at
• aggressive-sounding noises or exposure to anything that makes you feel uncomfortable
• being around someone who has treated you badly
• certain smells, tastes, or noises (mentalhealth.net)

Emotional rants happen when we have unresolved issues in our lives. One might say, "I can fix it." This is not true because if you could fix it, you would have! That's why it keeps coming up. Certain issues still do have emotional triggers attached to it like death. We hear the saying "time heals all wounds", and I found this to be true. Yet some situations have deeper scars than others. Some things are old and you will be able to talk about them without the emotional rants. This is how you know you have peace in the situation.

THE BUTTERFLY

It seems we spend the majority of our lives chasing happiness, going through transformation and trying to figure out this thing called life. It's sort of interesting, in a way, that the caterpillar spends most of its life going through transformation, only to spend a few days as a butterfly. The "healed" you is only a short part of your life because as humans, we are always hit with the unexpected. Yet as we learn to embrace life and enjoy every second, we can embrace our healed selves and live an abundant life. After going through so many changes, you might think, "Wow! I'm healed and now what? I'm so used to surviving. How do I live?"

Accomplish the things the scars held you back from, but do not be afraid to create new goals! Sometimes we don't realize how much our past experiences have affected our future goals. So it's time to have a new and different outlook on life. Scientists have discovered over 20,000 different species of butterflies. Being who God created you to be is different; you just have to be willing to accept the path God lays out for you.

-Marriage
-Having children /Adopting
-New career
-Traveling

These are all ideas we can consider, or even reset. It's never too late to reset who you are while you are living your best life. An interesting fact about a butterfly is its wings are transparent.

The wings of a butterfly are covered in a multitude of miniature scales – thousands of them. And those colors you see when a butterfly flits across your yard are the reflections of various colors through the scales. The wings themselves are made up of a protein called chitin, which is the same protein that forms an insect's exoskeleton. And much like an exoskeleton, chitin is transparent. (Suburban Exterminating)

If someone is transparent, this means the person cannot or does not hide or conceal anything. It means people who want to know who you are free to observe. A person who is transparent has no secrets and tells no lies. In our caterpillar state, we rush everything and suffer great consequences. Yet as a butterfly, we fly and show our beautiful Christ-like colors, drawing others to Christ for the up building of the kingdom.

Trusting and believing God's word will come to pass on the promises He has spoken. But they that wait upon the Lord shall renew their strength; they shall mount up with wings as eagles; they shall run, and not be weary; and they shall walk, and not faint. (Isaiah 40:31 KJV) Yes, this scripture speaks of eagles. But if we look at the caterpillar, it has to mount up with wings as well so it can become a new creature. This means that anyone who belongs to Christ has become a new person. The old life is gone; a new life has begun! (2 Corinthians 5:17 NIV)

Butterflies are very active during the day and visit a variety of wildflowers. As long as it is day, we must do the works of Him who sent us. Night is coming, when no one can work. Let's look at this in a deeper sense. Butterflies have only such a short life span and they use populations as a source to help flowers to bloom and grow. This scripture is simply saying live your best life in Christ; it will come a time we will die just like the butterfly. Yet our life spans do not just stop at a physical death. For the Lord Himself shall descend from heaven with a shout, with the voice of the archangel, and with the trump of God: and the dead in Christ shall rise first: Then we which are alive and remain shall be caught up together with them in the clouds, to meet the Lord in the air: and so shall we ever be with the Lord. (1 Thessalonians 4:16-17 NIV)

The desire for fulfillment is all our dreams. From the moment we are born, we recognize within ourselves an unquenchable hunger for more of life. We try to grasp onto every experience, enjoy every relationship, and maximize every opportunity. Even if we strive to fill our lives with adventure, we are never fully satisfied.

Referring back to the butterfly, its lifespan is short. This could be another way we can use the short lifespan of being a butterfly to teach us how to be grateful for the time and the things God has already graced us with. A life lived to the fullest is a life that is set apart by being in a relationship with Jesus, because He Himself is the definition of life. John 14:6 identify Jesus as the life. It reads, "Jesus answered, "I am the way and the truth and the life. No one comes to the Father except through Me." Christ is not only the life, but He is also the truth and the way in which we can have a fulfilling relationship with God the way we were designed to. I know it sounds hard, but we cannot pick and choose which parts of Jesus we accept and which we do not accept. Just in the same way that we cannot choose to be in a relationship with certain parts of any individual, we cannot live with Christ fully if we do not accept Him as the truth and the way, as well as the life.

Joy is an attitude or a belief, which soothes even in the most sorrowful of situations. Joy comes from within; it is an internal view. Joy, in the Biblical context, is not an emotion. It is not based on something positive happening in life, but is an attitude of the heart or spirit. Happiness is one of the many emotions that we have been given by God and we can accept it as one of His good gifts. However, like any other emotion, happiness is dependent on circumstances and can quickly fade away. It fades; things don't always go the way we plan. God may not guarantee us constant happiness when we begin a relationship with Him, but He does promise to be an ever-flowing source of joy. Joy knows and reminds us that our security is in our restored relationship with God and the eternal life He has promised us. It comes with knowing God and is based on His faithfulness.

I wanted to show you that we will spend a long time in the struggle state if we don't transform our minds. Even though the butterfly's life span is short, that doesn't stop it from transforming. But forget not this one thing, beloved, that one day is with the Lord as a thousand years, and a thousand years as one day. (2 Peter 3:8) With the transformation or change, one might say, "What's the point?" But if we really want to experience joy, we must start making the necessary changes to eliminate the weight and it might even shorten the wait.

The butterfly chapter is not as long as the caterpillar chapter. I would like to end this by saying that transformations in life can seem hard, and sometimes we have to keep moving. I press toward the mark for the prize of the high calling of God in Christ Jesus. (Philippians 3:14 KJV)

I want to deposit this in your spirit: you are worthy of everything God has for you! I speak life and healing to every sore place in your life. I speak peace and healing to those emotions that are out of control. I pray every visible scar heals properly. I speak life to every broken and forgotten dream. I speak life to every ounce of unforgiveness, whether you hold unforgiveness towards yourself, or toward others that want to hold you captive to your past. I pray that every need be supplied according to the word of God. I pray your faith be activated above material things and that you seek the things of God.

I prophetically speak that every door that is purposely locked in this season be unlocked and opened. I speak financial currency flow that is never-ending. I know you are blessed and I pray you continue to be blessed according to the word of God. Your thoughts are no longer bound by pain and shame. You shall no longer suffer in silence; you are free to live an abundant life. I pray if it's any sickness in your body, it shall dry up and line up according to the word of God. You are the head and not the tail. I decree and declare these words over your life. I decree and declare, according to the word that these words will penetrate down through your soul, in the name of Jesus!

As I sit here my mind goes to when Jesus was walking on the water. Immediately, Jesus made the disciples get into the boat and go on ahead of Him to the other side, while He dismissed the crowd. After He had dismissed them, He went up on a mountainside by Himself to pray. Later that night, He was there alone, and the boat was already a considerable distance from land, buffeted by the waves because the wind was against it. Shortly before dawn, Jesus went out to them, walking on the lake. When the disciples saw Him walking on the lake, they were terrified. "It's a ghost," they said, and cried out in fear.

But Jesus immediately said to them: "Take courage! It is I. Don't be afraid." "Lord, if it's You," Peter replied, "tell me to come to You on the water." "Come," He said. Then Peter got down out of the boat, walked on the water and came toward Jesus. But when he saw the wind, he was afraid and, beginning to sink, cried out, "Lord, save me!" Immediately, Jesus reached out His hand and caught him. "You of little faith," He said, "why did you doubt?" And when they climbed into the boat, the wind died down. Then those who were in the boat worshiped Him, saying, "Truly you are the Son of God." (Matthew 14:22-33 NIV)

Now! What in the world does this have to do with the butterfly? This passage shows a powerful demonstration on faith. It takes faith for us to undergo change. We can see the wonderful works of Jesus. Yet, it is hard for us to stay focused. In this scripture, the disciples saw Jesus walking on the sea and became afraid. Jesus replied to them, "Don't be afraid." Peter asked if he could come to Him.

The Bible says Peter began to walk to Jesus and began to sink. From experience, when I first became saved, I walked out on faith with my eyes on Jesus. But like Peter, I began to sink. When we transform in Christ, we tend to always keep trying to get everything done and become burned out. We have to learn to be like the butterfly-take a rest. Butterflies don't actually sleep. Instead, they rest, or become inactive at night or during the day when it's cloudy or cool.

We sink like Peter did because like Peter, we take our eyes off God and focus on the world and the things around us. We begin to sink. In our butterfly states, we have to remember not to take our eyes off God so we can continue to do the things of God. We have to be like Peter; when we realize we are sinking, we have to acknowledge it and ask God to save us. The Bible said after Jesus pulled Peter up, they began to worship God. We have to always remember to pray so we can continue to do the work of Christ like the butterfly does during pollination.

Another interesting fact about the butterfly is an old wise tale that says if human hands touch a butterfly, it can possibly shorten the butterfly life cycle. As long as a butterfly sticks to God's plans for it, the butterfly has a chance to live a longer life. If the butterfly gets off track, it might possibly come in contact with humans and could possibly shorten its lifespan . As long as we stick to the plan of God and be transformed by the renewing of the mind, we will have a long and prosperous life.

THINGS WE CAN LEARN FROM A BUTTERFLY

-Be Patient.

All good things come with time. We are growing, even when we cannot feel it. With great patience comes great rewards. "The end of something is better than its beginning. Patience is better than pride." (Ecclesiastes 7:8)

-Be Open To Change.

Be willing to be transformed. Without change, nothing beautiful would happen. You have to give up who you are to become who you might be. "To put off your old self, which belongs to your former manner of life and is corrupt through deceitful desires, and to be renewed in the spirit of your minds, and to put on the new self, created after the likeness of God in true righteousness and holiness." (Ephesians 4:22-24)

-Be Light And Free.

Enjoy life. When God opens a door, do not be afraid to move from one open door to the next. Look for peace in everything-the color, the humor and joy in every second God gives us.

I perceived that there is nothing better for them than to be joyful and to do good as long as they live; also that everyone should eat and drink and take pleasure in all his toil—this is God's gift to man. (Ecclesiastes 3:12-13)

-Be Spontaneous.

Go wherever your Godly wings take you. Fly forward in Jesus with love and confidence. Have the courage to experience new life opportunities. Walk in (love) and wisdom toward outsiders, making the best use of the time. (Colossians 4:5) **Make** the best use of the time, because the days are evil. (Ephesians 5:16)

-Be Conscious Of The Moment.

Look around and sight all of God's beautiful creations. Enjoy and smell the flowers, feel the sun and the breeze. The present moment is a gift for us to enjoy. Therefore, do not be anxious about tomorrow, for tomorrow will be anxious for itself. Sufficient for the day is its own trouble. (Matthew 6:34) Be sober-minded; be watchful. Your adversary the devil prowls around like a roaring lion, seeking someone to devour. (1 Peter 5:8)

I read something that was interesting when I was studying the caterpillar and the butterfly.

Some butterflies, such as the Monarch and Pipevine Swallowtail, eat poisonous plants as caterpillars and are poisonous themselves as adult butterflies. (Metal Mark Web Data)

Let's look at this in a spiritual sense. When we are going through hard times or trials and tribulations, it can make us bitter. When someone hurts us, it can make us become bitter towards others and cause us to treat people the way someone or others have treated us.

Earlier in the book we talked about how it is important not to miss a step during our transformation stage so we won't be spiritually bitter and our beautiful colors bleed all over the pollination stage of us drawing people to

Christ. The same way words can heal, they can also hurt and if the truth be told, we really don't know the damage we can cause. We can cause others' pollination process to be poisoned and instead of drawing people to Christ, we can push them away from Christ because we refused to heal. If we tell the truth, "hurt people" hurt people. A lying tongue hates its victims, and a flattering mouth works ruin. (Proverbs 26:28) It's very important to be aware of our own emotions and be willing to correct ourselves so we will build up the kingdom and not tear it down.

I hope something has been said in this book to edify you in the body of Christ and encourage you to keep the faith and hold fast to the words of God. I pray you will always remember Jeremiah 29:11: For I know the plans I have for you," declares the LORD, "plans to prosper you and not to harm you, plans to give you hope and a future. So encourage each other and build each other up, just as you are already doing" (1 Thessalonians 5:11).

-I see you now.

You are beautiful. You are worthy! The joy of the Lord has become your strength. When you lay down from your day to go to sleep, your body and mind rest and prepare themselves for a new day. When your feet hit the floor, I hear that "thank you Jesus!" joyfully being spoken from your mouth. Your mind is clear, your body and soul are full of energy. You are not anxious for nothing and you take everything to God in prayer and supplication, letting your requests be known to God. You can feel the presence of God all over and around you. You have understanding that exceeds the thoughts of man.

Yes, I see you. You are not being a trashcan for the world to dump all their never-ending problems on without wanting Jesus, for we know He is the great and ultimate healer. I see you! Resetting your life where it will work for you and not against you. I see you loving and living the life God designed for you to live. Yes, I see you no longer afraid to live your best life! Yes, I see you casting down every imagination that causes you to be stressed, overwhelmed and depressed. Yes, I see you living and not just existing. I believe in you!

Always remember, "The end of something is better than it's beginning. Patience is better than pride." (Ecclesiastes 7:8) I'm praying with you! Keep moving! I challenge you to pray and read the Bible at least one minute a day.

This sounds odd, but it will increase as you grow. We all have to start somewhere.

PRAYER

Lord, I thank you for being with your people. Lord, I thank you for the person who has deposited these words of knowledge in his/her mind and heart. Lord, I thank You that the words from this book have shown them areas of their lives that needed to be transformed. Lord, I thank you for opening every door that leads them to mental and spiritual freedom in Jesus. Lord, I pray every scar that was caused from going through transformations of life heals properly and their bodies line up according to the word that stress has triggered and caused illness that is illegal to the body. Jesus, You were wounded for our transgressions, you were bruised for our iniquities: the chastisement of our peace was upon you; and with your stripes we are healed. (Isaiah 53:5 KJV) I pray you rise up and be who He created you to be in your mother's wound. In Jesus' name I pray! Amen!

ACKNOWLEDGEMENTS

Giving all praises and thanks to my Lord and Savior, Jesus Christ, for giving me the strength and joy within (Nehemiah 8:10)!

I would like to thank my mother (Deloise Willoughby) for believing in me when I didn't believe in myself and not giving up on me. Thanks to my sister (April Willoughby) for showing me the true meaning of independence and Beauty Hatcher for listening to me cry when my heart was hurting.

Much love to John Davis, who taught me how to embrace change, even when I didn't believe change, was possible (he reminded me who I was in God). God will send people into your life for a time, a reason, and a season.

A special thanks to my son Bhristrian, my daughter Miracle ("Mia"), and my late and beloved daughter Chelsea for making me grow as a person. It's a privilege and an honor to be your mother!

Last, but not least, a special thank you to my niece, Kwa'Merias ("Mirra"), and nephews Ja'Meryn ("Jack") and Aah'Meryn ("Duke") for making me laugh, even when I wanted to cry. I love you guys!

A special thanks to the most praying man I know. Who poured into my spirit when I was at a crossroad in my life! P.C.B

9 798742 240457